A Note From Rick Renner

I am on a personal quest to see a "revival of the Bible" so people can establish their lives on a firm foundation that will stand strong and endure the test as end-time storm winds begin to intensify.

In order to experience a revival of the Bible in your personal life, it is important to take time each day to read, receive, and apply its truths to your life. James tells us that if we will continue in the perfect law of liberty — refusing to be forgetful hearers, but determined to be doers — we will be blessed in our ways. As you watch or listen to the programs in this series and work through this corresponding study guide, I trust you will search the Scriptures and allow the Holy Spirit to help you hear something new from God's Word that applies specifically to your life. I encourage you to be a doer of the Word He reveals to you. Whatever the cost, I assure you — it will be worth it.

> Thy words were found, and I did eat them;
> and thy word was unto me the joy and rejoicing of mine heart:
> for I am called by thy name, O Lord God of hosts.
> — Jeremiah 15:16

Your brother and friend in Jesus Christ,

Rick Renner

Real Faith vs. Fake Faith

Copyright © 2021 by Rick Renner
P.O. Box 702040
Tulsa, OK 74170

Published by Rick Renner Ministries
www.renner.org

ISBN 13: 978-1-68031-988-0

eBook ISBN 13: 978-1-68031-989-7

TOPIC

The Whole World Is Guilty Before God

SCRIPTURES

1. **James 2:10-13** — For whosoever shall keep the whole law, and yet offend in one point, he is guilty of all. For he that said, Do not commit adultery, said also, Do not kill. Now if thou commit no adultery, yet if thou kill, thou art become a transgressor of the law. So speak ye, and so do, as they that shall be judged by the law of liberty. For he shall have judgment without mercy, that hath shewed no mercy; and mercy rejoiceth against judgment.

2. **2 Corinthians 3:6** — ...The letter killeth, but the spirit giveth life.

3. **Romans 3:19,20** — ...That every mouth may be stopped, and all the world may become guilty before God. Therefore by the deeds of the law there shall no flesh be justified in his sight: for by the law is the knowledge of sin.

4. **Galatians 3:24** — Wherefore the law was our schoolmaster to bring us unto Christ, that we might be justified by faith.

5. **Galatians 3:26** — For ye are all the children of God by faith in Christ Jesus.

GREEK WORDS

1. "keep" — τηρέω (*tereo*): a watch of soldiers who were positioned to protect something important; soldiers who stood guard to keep watch

2. "whole" — ὅλος (*holos*): all; complete; entire; total; where we get the word whole

3. "law" — νόμος (*nomos*): with a definite article, THE law; here, it refers to all the laws and regulations contained in the Old Testament

4. "yet" — δὲ (*de*): remarkably

5. "offend" — πταίω (*ptaio*): err, fall, sin, stumble

6. "one point" — ἑνί (*heni*): one; one singular mistake in keeping every single law and regulation of the Old Testament

How To Use This Study Guide

This five-lesson study guide corresponds to *"Real Faith vs. Fake Faith"* *With Rick Renner* (Renner TV). Each lesson in this study guide covers a topic that is addressed during the program series, with questions and references supplied to draw you deeper into your own private study of the Scriptures on this subject.

To derive the most benefit from this study guide, consider the following:

First, watch or listen to the program prior to working through the corresponding lesson in this guide. (Programs can also be viewed at **renner.org** by clicking on the Media/Archives links.)

Second, take the time to look up the scriptures included in each lesson. Prayerfully consider their application to your own life.

Third, use a journal or notebook to make note of your answers to each lesson's Study Questions and Practical Application challenges.

Fourth, invest specific time in prayer and in the Word of God to consult with the Holy Spirit. Write down the scriptures or insights He reveals to you.

Finally, take action! Whatever the Lord tells you to do according to His Word, do it.

For added insights on this subject, it is recommended that you obtain Rick Renner's books *Dream Thieves: Overcoming Obstacles To Fulfill Your Dreams* and *The Point of No Return: Tackling Your Next New Assignment With Courage and Commonsense*. You may also select from Rick's other available resources by placing your order at **renner.org** or by calling 1-800-742-5593.

7. "guilty" — ἔνοχος (*enochos*): to ensnare; trapped; guilty

8. "all" — πάντων (*panton*): all, an all-inclusive term meaning all of it

9. "adultery" — μοιχός (*moichos*): to take something illegally; one who violates a marital commitment by having a sexual relationship outside the covenant of marriage; one who is guilty of indecent sexual behavior

10. "kill" — φονεύω (*phoneuo*): to intentionally murder; to commit intentional homicide

11. "judged" — from the word κρίνω (*krino*): a word that referred to a jury that had just handed down their final sentence in a court of law; a verdict or a final sentence pronounced as the result of a court trial; after all the evidence had been presented and the judge had examined all the facts, a final verdict was issued by the court

12. "shall be" — μέλλοντες (*mellontes*): about to be; soon to be

13. "killeth" — ἀποκτείνω (*apokteino*): to slaughter; to massacre; to ruthlessly kill; to torture; to outright slaughter; can denote a death sentence

14. "that" — ἵνα (*hina*): points to a special point; here is the reason why

15. "every" — πᾶν (*pan*): all, an all-inclusive term

16. "mouth" — στόμα (*stoma*): mouth; the point of a sword; here, verbal argument, verbal defense

17. "stopped" — φράσσω (*phrasso*): stopped; blocked; shut up; closed; sealed; in this case, every verbal argument or defense be stopped and sealed shut

18. "all" — πᾶς (*pas*): all, an all-inclusive term

19. "guilty" — ὑπόδικος (*hupodikos*): compound of ὑπό (*hupo*) and δίκη (*dike*); ὑπό (*hupo*) means under; and δίκη (*dike*) pictures a judicial verdict; compounded, one who is under an irreversible, legal verdict of guilt that has been passed down by the court; hence, one who has no defense and is under an irreversible judgment

20. "therefore" — διότι (*dioti*): consequently, therefore, or a surety; it leaves no room for optional debate; a final conclusion

21. "by the deeds of the law" — ἐξ ἔργων νόμου (*ex ergon nomou*): literally, out of the works of the law; pictures what is impossible for the law to produce

22. "justified" — δικαιόω (*dikaioo*): from δίκη (*dike*), referring to a judicial verdict; here, a verdict that declares one to be legally approved,

made right, or declared to be righteous by the court; to have an upright standing before a court of law; in this case, God is the judge, and the audience or Heaven is the court

23. "his sight" — ἐνώπιον (*enopion*): in front of his eyes; in front of his gazing eyes

24. "by the law" — διὰ γὰρ νόμου (*dia gar nomou*): by the agency of the law

25. "knowledge" — ἐπίγνωσις (*epignosis*): pictures one on top of his subject, so that he knows it like a professional; a person who possesses an in-depth knowledge of an object, person, or truth; a masterful and professional knowledge of a subject; one who is "on top" of a subject and has masterful knowledge about it

26. "schoolmaster to bring" — παιδαγωγός (*paidagogos*): instructor; an authorized teacher to educate a child and lead him or her to adulthood and to higher development; the law was legally appointed to bring us to a higher conclusion and more noble place

27. "children" — υἱοὶ (*huoi*): plural form of υἱός (*huois*); a son, by birth or adoption; one who shares the same nature as a father, and who possesses the legal rights to his father's inheritance

28. "by faith" — διὰ τῆς πίστεως (*dia tes pisteos*): through the agency of faith

29. "in" — ἐν (*en*): in; a fixed location; inside

SYNOPSIS

The five lessons in this study on *Real Faith vs. Fake Faith* will focus on the following topics:

- The Whole World Is Guilty Before God
- Real Faith Has Corresponding Actions
- Faith vs. Works
- The Example of Abraham's Faith
- The Example of Rahab's Faith

The emphasis of this lesson:

All of humanity stands guilty before God, and no argument or excuse can put us in right-standing with Him. The only way to be justified and

kill. This word also means *to torture* or *to outright slaughter* and can even denote *a death sentence.* That's what trying to live by the law does — it slaughters and ruthlessly kills a person. Anyone trying to get into right standing with God and make it to Heaven by keeping the law is in for a very torturous life.

All the World Is Guilty Before God

The apostle Paul also had much to say about trying to live by the law. For example, in Romans 3:19 he said, "Now we know that what things soever the law saith, it saith to them who are under the law: that every mouth may be stopped, and all the world may become guilty before God." Notice the phrase "that every mouth may be stopped." The word "that," which is the Greek word *hina,* points to *a special point* and seems to say, "Here is the reason why."

The word "every" in Greek is the all-inclusive term *pan,* indicating *all,* or *everyone who will ever live on earth.* The Bible says, "…That every mouth may be stopped…" (Romans 3:19). In Greek, the word "mouth" is *stoma,* which depicts one's *physical mouth* or *the point of a sword.* In context here, it indicates the mouth of a person who is trying to make a point. It denotes *a verbal argument* or *a verbal defense* that is *stopped.*

This word "stopped" in Greek is *phrasso,* and it describes *something that is stopped, blocked, shut up, closed,* or *sealed.* In this case, it refers to every *verbal argument* or *defense* people offer in order to be deemed righteous in God's sight and granted entrance into Heaven. This verse tells us there is no verbal argument or defense a person can give to be seen as righteous. Every mouth is *phrasso — stopped, blocked, shut up, or closed.* You have to be perfect and without sin to make it into Heaven, and no one can achieve that on their own. Jesus Christ is the only One who lived a perfect life, and the only way we can be seen as perfect is through applying the blood He shed for us to our lives.

In addition to every mouth being stopped, the Bible says, "…All the world may become guilty before God" (Romans 3:19). The word "all" here is the all-inclusive Greek term *pas,* meaning *all* or *every person who has ever lived.* And the word "guilty" is a translation of the Greek word *hupodikos,* which is a compound of the words *hupo* and *dike.* *Hupo* means *under,* and *dike* pictures *a judicial verdict.* When these words are compounded, it describes *one who is under an irreversible, legal verdict of guilt that has been passed down by the court.* Hence, it is *one who has no defense and is under an irreversible judgment.*

No One Is Justified by Doing the Law

Romans 3:20 goes on to say, "Therefore by the deeds of the law there shall no flesh be justified in his sight: for by the law is the knowledge of sin." Notice the opening word "therefore." It is the Greek word *dioti*, which means *consequently, therefore*, or *a surety*. It leaves no room for optional debate and denotes *a final conclusion.*

This brings us to the phrase "by the deeds of the law," which in Greek literally means *out of the works of the law* and pictures a person who is living and trying to perform all that the law commands in order to be made righteous — something that is impossible for the law to produce. Scripture says, "Therefore by the deeds of the law there shall no flesh be justified in his sight…" (Romans 3:20).

No flesh — which includes you and all of humanity — shall be *justified* by the deeds of the law. In Greek, the word "justified" is *dikaioo*, from the word *dike*, referring to *a judicial verdict*. Here, it describes *a verdict that declares one to be legally approved, made right, or declared to be righteous by the court*. It means *to have an upright standing before a court of law*. In this case, God is the judge, and the audience or Heaven is the court.

This verse tells us that no human being will be made right and legally approved in God's sight by trying to keep the law. The words "his sight" is the Greek word *enopion*, which means *in front of his eyes* or *in front of his gazing eyes*. When we stand in front of God, we're not going to be declared innocent on the basis of how well we obeyed God's law. Even if we were able to perform all the law requires except for one command, we would still be considered guilty of breaking all of it.

The Bible goes on to say, "…For by the law is the knowledge of sin" (Romans 3:20). The phrase "by the law" in Greek is *dia gar nomou*, and it means *by the agency of the law*. In other words, through the means of the law, we become fully aware and knowledgeable of sin. The Greek word for "knowledge" here is *epignosis*, and it pictures *one on top of his subject, so that he knows it like a professional*. This is *a person who possesses an in-depth knowledge of an object, person, or truth; a masterful and professional knowledge of a subject.* It is one who is "on top" of a subject and has masterful knowledge about it.

So Why Did God Give Us the Law?

If there's no way we can keep the law, why do we have it? The apostle Paul helps answer this question in Galatians 3:24, which says, "Wherefore the law was our schoolmaster to bring us unto Christ, that we might be justified by faith." The phrase "schoolmaster to bring" is a translation of the Greek word *paidagogos*, which describes *an instructor* or *an authorized teacher to educate a child and lead him or her to adulthood and to higher development*. The law was legally appointed to be our teacher and bring us to a higher conclusion and more noble place. By giving us the law, God enabled us to see how inadequate we are to live by His standards. Our inability to keep the law leads us and positions us to receive the Good News — that we can be justified by placing our faith in Jesus Christ.

Here again we see the word "justified" — the Greek word *dikaioo*. It is from the word *dike*, and it refers to *a judicial verdict that declares one to be legally approved, made right, or declared to be righteous by the court*. When we put our faith in the finished work of Jesus Christ — trusting in Him and the blood He shed to pay for our sins and redeem us out of Satan's slave market — we stand before the court of Heaven *upright, cleansed, and in right-standing with God*, the Judge of all the universe.

The apostle Paul goes on to say, "For ye are all the children of God by faith in Christ Jesus" (Galatians 3:26). The word "all" is again the Greek word *pas*, which is an all-inclusive term meaning *all*. This word tells us that every single person who puts his or her faith in Jesus becomes one of God's *children*. The word "children" in Greek is *huoi*, the plural form of *huois*, which describes *a son, by birth or adoption. It is one who shares the same nature as a father and who possesses the legal rights to his father's inheritance.*

The Bible says this rebirth and adoption into God's family comes "by faith," which in Greek is *dia tes pisteos*, and it means *through the agency of faith*. Being made a son or daughter of God has nothing to do with keeping the law. Yes, we should obey what the Word of God says in both the New and Old Testaments, but we can never be good enough to do all that the Scriptures tell us. We can only become God's children through the action of placing our faith *in Christ Jesus* — not through works. The word "in" here describes *a fixed location* and it is *inside Jesus Christ*. Friend that is *real faith*!

In our next lesson, we are going to examine what it means to put your faith to work.

STUDY QUESTIONS

Study to shew thyself approved unto God, a workman that
needeth not to be ashamed, rightly dividing the word of truth.
— 2 Timothy 2:15

1. Take some time to carefully reflect on Ephesians 2:4,5,8,9. What is the Holy Spirit showing you about your salvation in this passage? How important is faith, and where does faith come from (also consider Romans 12:3)?

2. Jesus Christ is the only One who lived a perfect life, and the only way we can be perfect in God's eyes is through applying His Blood to our lives. According to these verses, how important is the blood of Jesus? What does it provide for you?

   • Hebrews 9:11-14; 1 Peter 1:18,19

   • Matthew 26:28; Hebrews 9:22

   • Colossians 1:19,20

   • Hebrews 10:19-22

   • John 6:53-56

   • 1 John 1:7

PRACTICAL APPLICATION

But be ye doers of the word, and not hearers only,
deceiving your own selves.
— James 1:22

1. Are you diligently trying to live right and do good? Are you attempting every day to obey all of God's commands written in His Word? Have you discovered how impossible it is to live a perfect life? In what ways has trying to live by the law felt like torture or even a death sentence to you?

2. Imagine that you died today and were ushered into the very presence of God, and He asked you why He should allow you to enter Heaven.

What reason would you give Him? On what grounds do you have the right to spend eternity with Him?

TOPIC

Real Faith Has Corresponding Actions

SCRIPTURES

1. **James 2:14-16** — What doth it profit, my brethren, though a man say he hath faith, and have not works? can faith save him? If a brother or sister be naked, and destitute of daily food, and one of you say unto them, Depart in peace, be ye warmed and filled; notwithstanding ye give them not those things which are needful to the body; what doth it profit?

2. **Matthew 3:8** — Bring forth therefore fruits meet for repentance.

GREEK WORDS

1. "what" — τι (*ti*): what; pointing to the most minute and minuscule detail

2. "profit" — ὄφελος (*ophelos*): advantage; benefit; need; profit; usefulness

3. "brethren" — ἀδελφός (*adelphos*): a term used to describe two or more who were born from the same womb; an endearing term used to describe those of one's own family; later used in a military sense to depict brothers in battle; a comrade; hence, brotherhood

4. "though" — ἐὰν (*ean*): supposing

5. "say" — λέγω (*lego*): says; verbal talk

6. "hath" — ἔχω (*echo*): to have, hold, or possess; to embrace something; to have a grip; to have a masterful embrace or grip

7. "faith" — πίστις (*pistis*): the New Testament word for faith; the root describes one who is persuaded; conveys the idea of that which is faithful, reliable, loyal, and steadfast; pictures that which is trustworthy, dependable, dedicated, constant, reliable, unfailing, and

unwavering; an unchanging, constant, stable, unwavering belief or behavior; a rock-solid belief; convinced to the core

8. "have not works" — ἔργα δὲ μὴ ἔχῃ (*erga de me eche*): works, however, he strangely, remarkably, emphatically does not possess; works, on the other hand, he remarkably and categorically does not have, possess, or have a grip on at all

9. "can" — δύναται (*dunatai*): power; ability; in this case, does mere talk alone have the ability; about faith alone have the ability or power

10. "if" — ἐὰν (*ean*): if; supposing if

11. "brother" or "sister" — ἀδελφός (*adelphos*) or ἀδελφὴ (*adelphe*): a term used to describe two or more who were born from the same womb; an endearing term used to describe those of one's own family; later used in a military sense to depict brothers in battle; a comrade; hence, brotherhood

12. "be" — ὑπάρχω (*huparcho*): to exist; one who is existing

13. "naked" — γυμνός (*gumnos*): physically naked; lacking proper clothes; one in desperate physical need; living bare

14. "destitute" — λείπω (*leipo*): tense means continuously lacking; continuously behind; continuously living in deficit and need; even carries the idea of abandonment

15. "daily" — ἐφήμερος (*ephmeros*): upon the day; at the start of the day; at the outset of the day; something that comes on one at the start of each day

16. "food" — τροφή (*trophe*): what is needed for life, nourishment, physical maintenance and sustenance

17. "depart" — ὑπάγω (*hupago*): be on your way

18. "peace" — εἰρήνη (*eirene*): the cessation of war; conflict put away; a time of rebuilding and reconstruction after war has ceased; distractions removed; a time of prosperity; the rule of order in the place of chaos; a calm, inner stability that results in the ability to conduct oneself peacefully even in the midst of circumstances that would normally be traumatic or upsetting; it is the Greek equivalent for the Hebrew word shalom, which expresses the idea of wholeness, completeness or tranquility in the soul that is unaffected by outward circumstances or pressures

19. "warmed" — θερμαίνω (*thermaino*): to warm oneself; a sauna or Roman bathhouse; go enjoy yourself and relax

20. "filled" — χορτάζω (*chortadzo*): be filled with food to the point of satisfaction

21. "notwithstanding" — δὲ (*de*): used for emphasis; but, however, shockingly

22. "give... not" — μὴ δῶτε (*me dote*): you do NOT give; not is a strong negative tone

23. "needful" — ἐπιτήδειος (*epitedeios*): suitable for the necessity of living; necessary to go on living normally

24. "body" — σῶμα (*soma*): the natural, physical body

25. "what" — τι (*ti*): what; pointing to the most minute and minuscule detail

26. "profit" — ὄφελος (*ophelos*): advantage; benefit; need; profit; usefulness

SYNOPSIS

When Jesus addressed the Pharisees and Sadducees, He boldly called them *hypocrites*. Interestingly, He learned this word while He was growing up. History tells us that the city of Sepphoris, which was about three miles from Nazareth, was where Jesus' grandparents lived. And in Sepphoris, there was a theater where live performances were viewed by the public. Each actor who took to the stage was called a *hypocrite*. In Greek, this word describes *a person who wore a mask*. In those days, actors wore masks to pretend they were someone else. The part they played was not who they really were. Thus, the hypocrites who wore masks were great pretenders.

That's why Jesus called the Pharisees and Sadducees hypocrites. They were like actors playing the part of godly men, when in reality they were ungodly men who were putting on a good performance. They knew all the right words and lines to say, but their hearts were not in it.

Jesus said, "...The hour is coming, and now is, when the true worshipers will worship the Father in spirit and truth; for the Father is seeking such to worship Him" (John 4:23 *NKJV*). Friend, God doesn't want us to be actors who pretend to be something we are not. He wants us — His people — to live and love Him with a heart of real faith, not fake faith.

The emphasis of this lesson:

When a person possesses real faith, that faith will be moving him or her to do something, because faith always has corresponding actions. There

is absolutely no advantage or usefulness to our faith if it is void of good works. God desires real action — not lip service — from our lives.

As we continue our study in the book of James, we see him address the difference between fake faith and real faith by saying:

> What doth it profit, my brethren, though a man say he hath faith, and have not works? can faith save him? If a brother or sister be naked, and destitute of daily food, and one of you say unto them, Depart in peace, be ye warmed and filled; notwithstanding ye give them not those things which are needful to the body; what doth it profit?
>
> —James 2:14-16

In this passage, James begins to ask his readers some candid rhetorical questions that are very important. To really grasp the full meaning of what he is saying, let's back up and explore the meaning of some key words starting in verse 14.

'What Doth It Profit'

James opens with the word "what"— the little Greek word *ti*, which means *what* and points to *the most minute and minuscule detail.* The use of this word here is like an exclamation point. It is James' way of trying to get the attention of his readers. It is as if he is raising the intensity of his voice and saying, "What in the world does it profit...."

The word "profit" in Greek is *ophelos* — a word used all throughout the New Testament. It signifies *an advantage; a benefit; a need; a profit;* or *usefulness.* The use of this word tells us that real faith is *advantageous, beneficial, profitable,* and *useful.* James is amazed at what he is hearing about these believers and now he is challenging them to think about what they're doing.

James Addressed His Readers as 'Brethren'

At this point in James' letter, 42 verses have been written, and for the seventh time in those 42 verses, he calls his readers "brethren." Obviously, there is something very important about this salutation.

As we noted in our first two studies on the book of James, the word "brethren" is a translation of the Greek word *adelphos,* a term used to describe *two or more who were born from the same womb*. It is an endearing term used to describe *those of one's own family*. The use of this word tells us that James was not judging or condemning his readers. Instead, he was placing himself down in the trenches, side by side with them, speaking to them as their *equal*, not their superior.

Keep in mind, James was the half-brother of Jesus. No one was more visible than him, and yet he was willing to humble himself and come right down to the level of his readers. They were in the trenches, so he got down in the trenches with them. The fact is, James and everyone he was writing to were all born out of the womb of God, because they were all born of God.

Interestingly, this word "brethren," — the Greek word *adelphos* — was first popularized by Alexander the Great, who was the greatest soldier in the world during that period. From time to time when he held large award ceremonies to reward soldiers who had been especially brave, he would call them on the stage, place his arm around them, and with his other arm he would motion to all the other adoring soldiers and say, "Let all the empire know that Alexander is proud to be the brother (*adelphos*) of this soldier."

Thus, this term became known to depict *brothers in battle, comrades*, and *brotherhood*. It was an endearing classification that James used to connect with his readers who had endured much persecution but had remained in the fight of faith.

Faith Is More Than Just Talk

Looking again at James 2:14, it says, "What doth it profit, my brethren, though a man say he hath faith, and have not works? can faith save him?" The word "though" is the Greek word *ean*, which would best be translated as *supposing*. James said, "...*Supposing* a man say he hath faith...." The word "say" here is a form of the Greek word *lego*, which describes *verbal talk* or *conversation*, and the word "hath" is the Greek word *echo*, which means *to have, hold*, or *possess*. It carries the idea of *embracing something* or *having a masterful embrace or grip*.

Basically, James is painting a rhetorical picture of a person who is talking a mile a minute about his great faith. The word "faith" is the Greek word *pistis*, which is the New Testament word for *faith*. It describes *one who is persuaded* and conveys the idea of that which is *faithful, reliable, loyal*, and *steadfast*. It pictures *that which is trustworthy, dependable, dedicated, constant*, *reliable, unfailing,* and *unwavering.* Moreover, it depicts *an unchanging, constant, stable, unwavering belief or behavior, a rock-solid belief or one convinced to the core.*

Keep in mind that the word "faith" used in the New Testament describes a force that is moving forward. Faith never stays still or remains inactive; it is always moving and working to accomplish something. James is telling us that if a person truly holds, has, and possesses faith, that faith will be moving him or her to do something, because faith always has corresponding actions.

- Romans 12:3 says every man has a measure of faith.
- Romans 1:17 says the righteous live by faith.
- Ephesians 2:8,9 says we are saved through faith.
- Hebrews 11:7 says an active faith is essential to please God.
- 2 Corinthians 8:5-7 says we can abound in faith.
- 2 Thessalonians 1:3 says our faith can grow exceedingly.
- 1 John 5:4 says our faith has the ability to overcome the world.

Indeed, faith is like a bullet shot out of a gun. It carries great force and is aimed in a specific direction. When it hits the desired target, a noticeable, lasting impact is made.

Corresponding Actions Always Accompany Real Faith

Through James, the Holy Spirit is telling us that there is no benefit, no advantage, and no profit from merely saying we have and hold great faith. If we are all talk "...and have not works? can faith save [us]?" (James 2:14) In Greek, the phrase "have not works" is *erga de me eche,* and in the context here it literally means, *"Works, however, he strangely, remarkably, emphatically does not possess."* It could even be translated, *"Works, on the other hand, he remarkably and categorically does not have, possess, or have a grip on at all."*

Hence, there is no visible demonstration of faith in his life. To this, James asks the question, "Can faith save him?" The word "can" here is the Greek word *dunatai,* which describes *power and ability.* In this case, James is posing the question, "Does mere talk alone have the ability or the power to save?"

Remember, when Jesus talked to the Pharisees and Sadducees, He addressed them as *hypocrites*. They were like actors wearing theatrical masks playing the part of godly men but were really ungodly. When the Pharisees and Sadducees came to John the Baptist at the Jordan River to be baptized, he called them *vipers*. Although they knew the right religious lingo and had memorized the lines, the actions of their lives didn't demonstrate the faith they claimed to possess.

With a holy boldness, John told these hypocrites, "Bring forth therefore fruits meet for repentance" (Matthew 3:8). In other words, "Produce outward evidence or actions of the real faith you claim to possess." Again, real faith always has corresponding actions. If you claim to have faith but have no corresponding actions, something is flawed in your faith.

We Are To Care for Fellow Believers Who Are 'Naked and Destitute'

In order to make sure we really get the point, James continues presenting his hypothetical situation by saying, "If a brother or sister be naked, and destitute of daily food, and one of you say unto them, Depart in peace, be ye warmed and filled; notwithstanding ye give them not those things which are needful to the body; what doth it profit?" (James 2:15,16)

The word "if" that begins verse 15 is again the Greek word *ean*, which means *supposing*. James says, "Supposing a brother or sister...." The words "brother" or "sister" in Greek are *adelphos* and *adelphe*, terms used to describe *two or more who were born from the same womb*. James used these endearing terms to denote brothers and sisters in Christ born from the womb of God — *comrades* or *brothers* in battle.

He said, "Suppose they *be* naked...." The word "be" is the Greek word *huparcho*, which means *to exist* and describes *one who is continually existing in a particular state*. In this case, the brother or sister is "naked." This word is a form of the Greek word *gumnos*, meaning *physically naked*. It is *one lacking proper clothes* or *one in desperate physical need*. It could also be translated as *living bare*.

In addition to being *naked*, these fellow believers are also "destitute." This word is derived from the Greek word *leipo*, and the tense means *continuously lacking*, *continuously behind*; or *continuously living in deficit and need*. It even carries the idea of *abandonment*.

Specifically, James says they are continuously lacking "daily food." The word "daily" is a translation of the Greek word *ephmeros*, which means *upon* or *at the start of the day*. In other words, the moment this person awakens at the outset of their day, they are *deficient of food*. The word "food" is the Greek word *trophe*, and it describes *what is needed for life, nourishment, physical maintenance and sustenance*.

These brothers and sisters in James' example are not just lacking desserts and extra frills. They are lacking the basic necessities for daily existence and are really in trouble.

Real Action — Not Lip Service — Is What God Desires

James said that if we see a brother or sister in such a situation, "And one of you say unto them, Depart in peace, be ye warmed and filled; notwithstanding ye give them not those things which are needful to the body; what doth it profit?" (James 2:16).

The word "depart" here is the Greek word *hupago*, which basically means *be on your way*. Then he adds "in peace." In Greek, the word "peace" is *eirene*, and it describes *the cessation of war* or *the putting away of conflict*. It is the Greek equivalent for the Hebrew word *shalom*, which expresses the idea of *wholeness, completeness* or *tranquility in the soul that is unaffected by outward circumstances or pressures*.

Therefore this phrase "Depart in peace" is the equivalent of saying, "Be at peace! Get up and get moving because everything is going to be just fine. The conflict is over, and a time of prosperity and rebuilding is here. Relax and be whole and complete in every part of your life." How would you react if a fellow believer told you this and you were destitute and continually lacking essential daily provisions?

How about if they smiled and said, "Be ye warmed and filled"? The word "warmed" in James 2:16 is the Greek word *thermaino*, which means *to warm oneself* and is the very word used to describe *a sauna* or *Roman bathhouse*. The use of this word is the equivalent of someone saying, "Go enjoy yourself, relax, and be filled." This word "filled" in Greek means *to be filled with food to the point of satisfaction*. How could anyone be filled to the point of satisfaction if they had no food to eat? It simply makes no sense.

We Are Called To Meet Each Other's Needs

Then James says, "...Notwithstanding ye give them not those things which are needful to the body; what doth it profit?" (James 2:16). In Greek, "notwithstanding" is the word *de*, which could be translated *remarkably*, *shockingly*, or *however*. It is used here for emphasis.

James said, "*Shockingly*, you give them not those things which are needful to the body...." The words "give... not" are a translation of the Greek words *me dote*, meaning *you do NOT give*, and the word "not" is in a strong, emphatic negative tone. The people in James' example didn't give what was "needful" — the Greek word *epitedeios*, which means *suitable for the necessity of living* or *necessary to go on living normally*. And the word "body" is the Greek word *soma*, which describes *the natural, physical body*.

Basically, James called out these believers for having the resources and ability to help their fellow Christians in need, but all they did was offer them placating lip service. To this he said, "...What doth it profit?" (James 2:16). The word "what" is again the little Greek word *ti*, which describes *the most minute and minuscule detail*. It is like a huge exclamation point saying, "What is this?! What tiny spec of profit does this bring?!"

The word "profit" is again the Greek word *ophelos*, which describes *an advantage, a benefit, a need, a profit*, or *usefulness*. The point James is pounding home is that real faith has actions that help people. It is way more than just cute Christian clichés or a mouthful of good wishes. Talk itself is not going to change anyone's situation. It is divinely directed actions that make the difference, which is what we will focus on in our next lesson.

STUDY QUESTIONS

Study to shew thyself approved unto God, a workman that needeth not to be ashamed, rightly dividing the word of truth.
— 2 Timothy 2:15

1. The way to touch and warm God's heart is to care for the people He brings across your path. Take a few moments to look up First John 3:17,18 in a few different Bible versions. Then write down and commit to memory the rendering of this verse that impacts you most.

2. Helping those in need is a principle found all throughout Scripture, including Galatians 6:10 and Hebrews 13:16. Carefully reflect on these two verses and jot down what the Holy Spirit reveals to you.

PRACTICAL APPLICATION

> **But be ye doers of the word, and not hearers only,**
> **deceiving your own selves.**
> **—James 1:22**

1. If you truly possess real faith, your faith will be moving you to do something. What is your faith moving you to do right now? What corresponding actions confirm to God and others that you are living by faith?

2. Seven times in his first two chapters, James addressed his readers as "brethren," which is the Greek word *adelphos*, describing *two or more who were born from the same womb*. Who are you doing life with that you would call your brother or sister in Christ? How has their comradery and friendship been a source of strength to you?

3. How would you react if you were destitute and continually lacking essential daily provisions and a fellow believer told you, "Be at peace! Get up and get moving because everything's going to be just fine! The conflict is over, and a time of prosperity is here. Relax and enjoy your life"?

4. Do you know of a brother or sister in Christ who is "naked and destitute of daily food"? That is, they are *continually lacking proper clothes, daily food*, or *living bare and in desperate physical need*. Who is it? What actions can you begin to take to care for them?

LESSON 3

TOPIC

Faith vs. Works

SCRIPTURES

1. **2 Timothy 1:5** — When I call to remembrance the unfeigned faith that is in thee....

2. **1 Thessalonians 1:3** — Remembering without ceasing your work of faith....

3. **James 2:16-20** — And one of you say unto them, Depart in peace, be ye warmed and filled; notwithstanding ye give them not those things which are needful to the body; what doth it profit? Even so faith, if it hath not works, is dead, being alone. Yea, a man may say, Thou hast faith, and I have works: shew me thy faith without thy works, and I will shew thee my faith by my works. Thou believest that there is one God; thou doest well: the devils also believe, and tremble. But wilt thou know, O vain man, that faith without works is dead?

GREEK WORDS

1. "what" — τι (*ti*): what; pointing to the most minute and minuscule detail

2. "profit" — ὄφελος (*ophelos*): advantage; benefit; need; profit; usefulness

3. "even so" — οὕτως (*houtos*): in this manner; in this way; in accordance with this; along this line

4. "faith" — πίστις (*pistis*): the New Testament word for faith; the root describes one who is persuaded; conveys the idea of that which is faithful, reliable, loyal, and steadfast; pictures that which is trustworthy, dependable, dedicated, constant, reliable, unfailing, and unwavering; an unchanging, constant, stable, unwavering belief or behavior; a rock-solid belief; convinced to the core

5. "have not works" — ἔργα δὲ μὴ ἔχῃ (*erga de me eche*): works, however, he strangely, remarkably, emphatically does not possess; works, on the other hand, he remarkably and categorically does not have, possess, or have a grip on at all

6. "dead" — νεκρός (*nekros*): a lifeless corpse; a cadaver with no life left in it; a body disconnected to life; a corpse

7. "yea" — Ἀλλ' (*all'*): But, on the one hand

8. "may say" — ἐρεῶ (*ereo*): rhetorically a man may say; where we get the word rhetoric; denotes an imagined conversation; let's imagine one man addressing another and saying

9. "Thou" — Σὺ (*Su*): direct speech; You!

10. "hast" — ἔχω (*echo*): to have, hold, or possess

11. "and I" — κἀγὼ (*kago*): and I on the other hand

12. "have" — ἔχω (*echo*): to have, hold, or possess

13. "works" — ἔργα (*erga*): works, deeds, or activity, outward accompanying actions; outward proof and evidence of faith

14. "shew" — δείκνυμι (*deiknumi*): something outwardly observable or done visibly to authenticate, prove, or guarantee something to onlookers; to prove by showing; to display; to show off; to vividly portray; to point out; to illustrate; to make a vivid presentation; to demonstrate

15. "thy faith" — τὴν πίστιν σου (*ten pistin sou*): with a definite article; the faith of yours; making a comparison

16. "without" — χωρὶς (*choris*): to be outside of something, such as someone who lives outside the perimeters of a city; a comparison between being outside or inside something; depicts someone who is out of, not in, a specific location; primarily, to be on the outside

17. "shew" — δείκνυμι (*deiknumi*): something outwardly observable or done visibly to authenticate, prove, or guarantee something to onlookers; to prove by showing; to display; to show off; to vividly portray; to point out; to illustrate; to make a vivid presentation; to demonstrate

18. "by" — ἐκ (*ek*): out of; out of the midst of; meaning there is something visible to see; there is outward proof that is tangible

19. "thou believest" — σὺ πιστεύεις (*su pisteueis*): direct speech; you believe, almost as a question or speculation

20. "doest" — ποιέω (*poieo*): do; tense means, you are doing

21. "well" — καλός (*kalos*): good or beautifully; super; superb

22. "devils" — δαιμόνιον (*daimonion*): evil spirits, demons, devils

23. "also" — καί (*kai*): also; additionally

24. "believe" — πίστις (*pistis*): the New Testament word for faith; a rock-solid belief; convinced to the core

25. "tremble" — φρίσσω (*phrisso*): pictures trembling or tremors; to shudder; to be struck with extreme fear; to be horrified; to be panicked

26. "vain" — κενός (*kenos*): depicts something that is empty, void, or wasted; can denote emptiness or shallowness; empty head; shallow thinker

27. "that" — ὅτι (*hoti*): points to a concrete conclusion

28. "without" — χωρὶς (*choris*): to be outside of something, such as someone who lives outside the perimeters of a city; a comparison between being outside or inside something; depicts someone who is out of, not in, a specific location; primarily, to be on the outside

29. "works" — ἔργα (*erga*): works, deeds, or activity, outward accompanying actions

30. "dead" — ἀργός (*argos*): incorrect rendering; original says unprofitable, lazy, worthless, unprovable; even injurious

SYNOPSIS

In our second lesson, we noted that Jesus called the Pharisees and Sadducees *hypocrites*. They were like actors who wore theatrical masks, pretending to be something they were not. They had memorized all the religious lines and could speak the scriptural lingo in order to please their audience. But their faith was fake.

Interestingly, Paul used the same Greek word for *hypocrisy* in his second letter to his spiritual son Timothy. Regarding Timothy's character, Paul said, "When I call to remembrance the unfeigned faith that is in thee…" (2 Timothy 1:5). The word "unfeigned" here means *without hypocrisy*. Unlike the Pharisees and Sadducees, Timothy didn't wear a spiritual mask. He had real faith, and his actions proved it.

Like Timothy, the believers in Thessalonica also had real faith. Paul called attention to it in First Thessalonians 1:3, saying, "Remembering without ceasing your work of faith…." Interestingly, the Greek text here literally says, "Remembering without ceasing *your work produced by faith*…." Indeed, real faith is always accompanied by corresponding works, which we will see clearly in this lesson.

The emphasis of this lesson:

A mouthful of faith-filled platitudes doesn't equal genuine faith. Real faith always has actions to back it up. Faith in words only with no actions resembles a lifeless corpse. Even demons believe in God — and tremble. If our faith isn't accompanied by actions, we're in the same category as demons. When real faith is operating, there's always something visible to see.

Actions Speak Louder Than Words

As we wrapped up Lesson 2, we examined James' words in James 2:16, where he said, "And one of you say unto them, Depart in peace, be ye warmed and filled; notwithstanding ye give them not those things which are needful to the body; what doth it profit?"

Essentially, James is letting us know that a mouthful of faith-filled platitudes does not equal genuine faith. Real faith always has actions to back it up. If we know that a brother or sister in Christ is destitute of the daily essentials for living, and merely bid them, "Blessings and peace," James said, "…What doth it profit?" (James 2:16).

The word "what" here is the little Greek word *ti*, which describes *the most minute and minuscule detail*. This word serves as a huge exclamation point saying, "What! What ounce of profit does this bring?!" We saw that the word "profit" is the Greek word *ophelos*, which describes *an advantage, a benefit, a need, a profit*, or *usefulness*. When real faith is in action, there's an advantage, a benefit, a profit, and a usefulness that results. Words alone don't bring change. Tangible actions are what make the difference.

Faith Without Works Is Dead

James continues to elaborate on the importance of works by saying:

> **Even so faith, if it hath not works, is dead, being alone. Yea, a man may say, Thou hast faith, and I have works: shew me thy faith without thy works, and I will shew thee my faith by my works. Thou believest that there is one God; thou doest well: the devils also believe, and tremble. But wilt thou know, O vain man, that faith without works is dead?**
> **—James 2:17-20**

First of all, James tells us, "Even so faith, if it hath not works, is dead, being alone" (James 2:17). Notice the words "even so." They are a translation of the Greek word *houtos*, which means *in this manner, in this way, in accordance with this*, or *along this line*. After all James has said in previous verses about the need for action to accompany words, he basically said, "In accordance with all this, faith, if it hath not works, is dead, being alone."

The word "faith" here is the Greek word *pistis*, which is the New Testament word for *faith*. It describes *one who is solidly persuaded* and conveys the idea of *one that is faithful, reliable, loyal*, and *steadfast*. It pictures *one that is trustworthy, dependable, dedicated, constant, reliable, unfailing, and unwavering*. This word *pistis* depicts faith that is *an unchanging, constant, stable, unwavering belief or behavior.* It is *a rock-solid belief* or *someone convinced to the core.*

What does the Bible say about faith?

- Romans 12:3 says every man has a measure of faith. The word "every" is all-encompassing and means *every single person who was and will ever be alive on the earth* has a measure of faith given to them by God.

- Romans 1:17 says the righteous live by faith, which means if we're going to really live as Christ intended, we're going to have to walk by faith and not by what we feel and see.

- Ephesians 2:8,9 says we are saved through faith in Christ, not by the good deeds we do.

- Hebrews 11:6 says an active faith is essential to please God. When we stand on the promises He gave us and actively engage in what He's called us to do, He is pleased greatly.

- 2 Corinthians 8:5-7 says we can abound in faith.

- 2 Thessalonians 1:3 says our faith can grow exceedingly.

- 1 John 5:4 says our faith has the ability to overcome the world and override all its systems.

In each of these verses, the word "faith" is the Greek word *pistis*, and it *describes something that is in movement.* Remember, faith is not stationary nor is it silent. Like a bullet that is shot out of a gun, faith is a powerful force that is in movement and always producing. It is aimed at a specific target and always makes a powerful impact when it achieves its purpose. Friend, it's not enough just to *say* you have faith. If you have no accompanying works, then you're not moving in faith.

Faith Outside of Works
Is Like a Lifeless Corpse

Looking again at James 2:17, it says, "Even so faith, if it hath not works, is dead, being alone." Take note of the word "if." Again it is the Greek word *ean*, which means *supposing*. It is the equivalent of James saying, "*Supposing* a person says they have faith, but hath not works...." The phrase "have not works," in Greek is *erga de me eche*, and would be better translated as, "*Works, however, he strangely, remarkably, emphatically does not possess,*" or *"Works, on the other hand, he remarkably and categorically does not have, possess, or have a grip on at all."*

Faith that doesn't have accompanying works is *dead*. The word "dead" here is the Greek word *nekros*, which describes *a lifeless corpse*. It is *a cadaver with no breath or life left in it; a body disconnected from life; a corpse*. That is what faith in words only with no actions resembles — *a lifeless corpse*. Therefore, when real faith is present, works accompany it.

A Comparison Between Real and Fake Faith

In the next verse, James goes on to say, "Yea, a man may say, Thou hast faith, and I have works: shew me thy faith without thy works, and I will shew thee my faith by my works" (James 2:18).

The word "yea" is the Greek word *all*, and here it means *"But, on the one hand."* The phrase "may say" in Greek is *ereo*, which is from where we get the word *rhetoric*. It is the equivalent of saying, "Rhetorically, a man may say...." This word *ereo* denotes *an imagined conversation*. It is as if James is telling us, "Let's imagine one man addressing another and saying, 'Thou hast faith....'"

The word "Thou" is the Greek word *Su*, and it signifies *very direct speech*. It is an emphatic, "You!" This takes us to the word "hast," which is the Greek word *echo*, meaning *to have, hold, or possess*. This man is boldly declaring, "You claim to have, hold, and possess faith, and I have works...." The phrase "and I" is the Greek word *kago*, which means, *"And I, on the other hand*, have works." The word "have" is once again the Greek word *echo*, meaning *to have, hold, or possess*. What did the first man say the second man had and possessed? "Works" — the Greek word *erga*, which denotes *works, deeds, activity*, or *outward accompanying actions*. These "works" are *outward proof and evidence of faith*.

In James' example, the first man said, "...Shew me thy faith without thy works, and I will shew thee my faith by my works" (James 2:18). The word "shew," which appears twice in this verse, is the Greek word *deiknumi*, and it describes *something outwardly observable or done visibly to authenticate, prove, or guarantee something to onlookers*. It means *to prove by showing; to display; to show off; to vividly portray; to point out; to illustrate; to make a vivid presentation;* or *to demonstrate*.

Basically, this man is saying, "Demonstrate thy faith without thy works." In Greek, "thy faith" is *ten pistin sou*, which includes a definite article, and it means *the faith of yours*. He is making a comparison. The word "without" is the Greek word *choris*, which means *to be outside of something*, such as someone who lives outside the perimeters of a city. This is *a comparison between being outside or inside something*. The use of this word *choris* (without) is the equivalent of saying, "You say you have faith, but if you don't have works, you're living outside of faith and not in faith.

The comparison continues as the man comes back and says, "…I will shew thee my faith by my works" (James 2:18). Again, the word "shew" in Greek is *deiknumi*, and it depicts *something outwardly observable or done visibly to authenticate, prove, or guarantee something to onlookers*. He is going to prove by showing, displaying, vividly portraying, and illustrating his faith by his works.

The word "by" here is the Greek word *ek*, which means *out of* or *out of the midst of*. This word indicates there is something visible to see — there is outward proof that is tangible. When real faith is in operation, there is always something visible to see. Real faith is accompanied by action that produces results.

Even Demons Believe in God — and Tremble

When we come to James 2:19, it says, "Thou believest that there is one God; thou doest well: the devils also believe, and tremble." In Greek, the phrase "thou believest" is *su pisteueis*, which is very direct speech. It is as if the person speaking is suspicious and asks the question, "So you say you believe, do you?"

Then he says, "…Thou doest well…." The word "doest" is the Greek word *poieo*, which means *do*, but the tense here indicates, *you are doing*. The word "well" is the Greek word *kalos*, and it means *good, beautifully, super*, or *superb*. Taken together, James is saying, "So you say you believe, do you? Well, you're doing pretty good. But the devils also believe and tremble."

The word "devils" is a translation of the Greek word *daimonion*, which describes *evil spirits, demons, or devils*. James said that evil spirits and demons "believe," which is the Greek word *pistis*, the New Testament word for *faith*. Amazingly, demonic spirits have a *rock-solid belief* and are *convinced to the core* that there is one God. In fact, their faith is so intense they "tremble" at the thought of Him.

In Greek, the word "tremble" is *phrisso*, and it pictures *trembling* or *tremors*. It means *to shudder*, *to be struck with extreme fear*, *to be horrified*, or *to be panicked*. This is exactly how the demons reacted when Jesus showed up on the scene. The gospels record they were terrified of Jesus and begged Him not to torment them before their appointed time of judgement.

Faith Apart From Works Is
Unprofitable, *Worthless*, and *Unprovable*

James 2:20 is basically a restatement of what is declared in verse 17 with an expanded meaning. It says, "But wilt thou know, O vain man, that faith without works is dead?" The word "vain" here is the Greek word *kenos*, and it depicts *something that is empty, void,* or *wasted*. It can denote *emptiness* or *shallowness*, and in this verse it describes *an empty head* or *shallow thinker*.

A literal translation of this passage would be, "Wilt thou know, O empty-headed shallow thinker, that faith without works is dead." Even the word "that" is significant here. It is the Greek word *hoti*, which points to *a very important, concrete conclusion*. The word "without" is the Greek word *choris*, the same word we saw in verse 18, and it means *to be outside of something*, such as someone who lives outside the perimeters of a city. Thus, James is saying, "Faith existing outside of or apart from works is dead."

The word "works" is again the Greek word *erga*, which describes *works, deeds, activity,* or *outward accompanying actions*. The big difference here is the meaning of the word "dead." It is not *nekros*, as we saw in verse 17. Instead, it is the Greek word *argos*, which means *unprofitable, lazy, worthless, unprovable,* or *even injurious*. Why is it considered injurious? Because when people say, "My faith is private and not something I demonstrate in public," it gives others the wrong impression of what faith is. Real faith has outward actions and is profitable. Faith "without" (*or outside of*) works is dead (*argos*) — it is *unprofitable, lazy, worthless,* and *unprovable*.

In our next lesson, we will take a close-up view at the life of Abraham and see what real faith in action looks like.

STUDY QUESTIONS

Study to shew thyself approved unto God, a workman that
needeth not to be ashamed, rightly dividing the word of truth.
— 2 Timothy 2:15

1. Just before giving us a model of how we should pray, Jesus tells us
   how to not operate in fake faith like the hypocrites. Carefully read
   His words in Matthew 6:1-8 and describe what real faith looks like in
   regard to *giving* and *praying*.
2. According to Mark 5:1-13 and Luke 8:26-32, how did the legion of
   demons living in the demoniac react when Jesus arrived on the scene,
   and what did they say to Him? (Also consider Mark 1:23-26.)
3. In contrast, what did the demon say and do when the seven sons of
   Sceva attempted to cast him out (*see* Acts 19:13-16)? What does this
   say to you about the kind of faith the sons of Sceva were operating in?

PRACTICAL APPLICATION

But be ye doers of the word, and not hearers only,
deceiving your own selves.
— James 1:22

1. In your own words, describe the difference between *real faith* and *fake
   faith*. Which one would you say you tend to operate in most often?
   What evidence in your life validates your answer?
2. Have you ever heard someone say, "My faith is private and not something I demonstrate in public"? How have you seen this type of faith
   give God a bad name and give others the wrong impression of what
   faith really is?
3. Remember: Real faith has outward actions and is profitable. Faith
   "without" (*or outside of*) works is dead (*argos*) — it is *unprofitable*, *lazy*,
   worthless, and *unprovable*.

TOPIC

The Example of Abraham's Faith

SCRIPTURES

1. **James 2:19-24** — Thou believest that there is one God; thou doest well: the devils also believe, and tremble. But wilt thou know, O vain man, that faith without works is dead? Was not Abraham our father justified by works, when he had offered Isaac his son upon the altar? Seest thou how faith wrought with his works, and by works was faith made perfect? And the scripture was fulfilled which saith, Abraham believed God, and it was imputed unto him for righteousness: and he was called the Friend of God. Ye see then how that by works a man is justified, and not by faith only.

2. **Genesis 22:2-13** — And he said, Take now thy son, thine only son Isaac, whom thou lovest, and get thee into the land of Moriah; and offer him there for a burnt offering upon one of the mountains which I will tell thee of. And Abraham rose up early in the morning, and saddled his ass, and took two of his young men with him, and Isaac his son, and clave the wood for the burnt offering, and rose up, and went unto the place of which God had told him. Then on the third day Abraham lifted up his eyes, and saw the place afar off. And Abraham said unto his young men, Abide ye here with the ass; and I and the lad will go yonder and worship, and come again to you. And Abraham took the wood of the burnt offering, and laid it upon Isaac his son; and he took the fire in his hand, and a knife; and they went both of them together. And Isaac spake unto Abraham his father, and said, My father: and he said, Here am I, my son. And he said, Behold the fire and the wood: but where is the lamb for a burnt offering? And Abraham said, My son, God will provide himself a lamb for a burnt offering: so they went both of them together. And they came to the place which God had told him of; and Abraham built an altar there, and laid the wood in order, and bound Isaac his son, and laid him on the altar upon the wood. And Abraham stretched forth his hand, and took the knife to slay his son. And the angel of the Lord called unto him out of heaven, and said, Abraham, Abraham: and he said,

Here am I. And he said, Lay not thine hand upon the lad, neither do thou any thing unto him: for now I know that thou fearest God, seeing thou hast not withheld thy son, thine only son from me. And Abraham lifted up his eyes, and looked, and behold behind him a ram caught in a thicket by his horns: and Abraham went and took the ram, and offered him up for a burnt offering in the stead of his son.

GREEK WORDS

1. "thou believest"— σὺ πιστεύεις (*su pisteueis*): direct speech; you believe, almost as a question or speculation

2. "well"— καλός (*kalos*): good or beautifully; super; superb

3. "devils"— δαιμόνιον (*daimonion*): evil spirits, demons, devils

4. "also"— καί (*kai*): also; additionally

5. "believe"— πίστις (*pistis*): the New Testament word for faith; a rock-solid belief; convinced to the core

6. "tremble"— φρίσσω (*phrisso*): pictures trembling or tremors; to shudder; to be struck with extreme fear; to be horrified; to be panicked

7. "vain"— κενός (*kenos*): depicts something that is empty, void, or wasted; can denote emptiness or shallowness; empty head; shallow thinker

8. "that"— ὅτι (*hoti*): points to a concrete conclusion

9. "without"— χωρὶς (*choris*): to be outside of something, such as someone who lives outside the perimeters of a city; a comparison between being outside or inside something; depicts someone who is out of, not in, a specific location; primarily, to be on the outside

10. "works"— ἔργα (*erga*): works, deeds, or activity, outward accompanying actions

11. "dead"— ἀργός (*argos*): incorrect rendering; original says unprofitable, lazy, worthless, unprovable; even injurious

12. "justified"— δικαιόω (*dikaioo*): from δίκη (*dike*), referring to a judicial verdict; here, a verdict that declares one to be legally approved, made right, or declared to be righteous by the court; to have an upright standing before a court of law; in this case, God is the judge, and the audience or Heaven is the court

13. "offered"— ἀναφέρω (*anaphero*): carries the idea of a sacrifice that is premeditated, carefully carried out, and performed with intention; thus, when Abraham brought his sacrificial offering to God, it was a

sacrifice following premeditated planning and determined intention to give what God asked him to surrender

14. "his son" — τὸν υἱὸν αὐτοῦ (*ton huion autou*): υἱός (*huois*), a son, by birth or adoption; one who shares the same nature as a father, and who possesses the legal rights to his father's inheritance; here, with a definite article, THE son of his

15. "upon" — ἐπί (*epi*): literally upon or on top of

16. "altar" — θυσιαστήριον (*thusiasterion*): an altar for slaying and burning of a sacrificial animal; a meeting place between God and a worshiper; a holy point of consecration and surrender;

17. "seest" — βλέπω (*blepo*): to watch, to see, to behold, to be aware; often intended to jolt and jar a listener or viewer to perk up and really listen to what is being said or to what is being seen

18. "how" — ὅτι (*hoti*): that; points to a conclusion

19. "faith" — πίστις (*pistis*): the New Testament word for faith; the root describes one who is persuaded; a rock-solid belief; convinced to the core

20. "wrought with" — συνεργέω (*sunergeo*): tense, working with; meaning to cooperate with; to work together with; to assist with; pictures two or more people or components working together to mutually accomplish a task

21. "and by works" — καὶ ἐκ τῶν ἔργων (*kai ek ton ergon*): and out of the midst of works; and in participation with works

22. "made perfect" — τελειόω (*teleioo*): to reach its end; to reach the end-aim; to function at full strength; to become full-grown; pictures transitioning from being youthful and immature to one who is full-grown and mature; denotes spiritually mature individuals who are living in accordance with the will of God

23. "believed" — πίστις (*pistis*): the New Testament word for faith; the root describes one who is persuaded; a rock-solid belief; convinced to the core

24. "imputed" — λογίζομαι (*logidzomai*): to mathematically count, calculate, or tabulate or to make a conclusion; used early in the bookkeeping world to portray the idea of a balance sheet or a profit-and-loss statement that a bookkeeper prepared at the end of the month or year; to make a calculation; to count, decide, deem, impute, reckon

25. "righteousness" — δικαιοσύνη (*dikaiosune*): from δίκη (*dike*), a judicial verdict; here, a verdict that declares one to be legally approved, made right, or declared to be righteous by the court; to have an upright standing before a court of law; in this case, God is the judge, and the audience or Heaven is the court; the Great Judge and the Court of Heaven imputed him to a status of approval and righteousness

26. "called" — καλέω (*kaleo*): past tense; called or invited; called by others

27. "friend" — φίλος (*philos*): friend; someone dearly loved and prized in a personal, intimate way; a trusted confidant; one held dear in a close bond of personal affection; a highly valued friend; a close associate

28. "see" — ὁράω (*horao*): to see; behold; perceive; delightfully view; to look with the intent to examine; to fully view; to experience; to know from personal observation

29. "that" — ὅτι (*hoti*): points to a conclusion

30. "by works" — ἐξ ἔργων (*ex ergon*): out of works; out of the midst of works; in the midst of works

31. "justified" — δικαιόω (*dikaioo*): also from δίκη (*dike*), a judicial verdict; here, a verdict that declares one to be legally approved, made right, or declared to be righteous by the court; to have an upright standing before a court of law; in this case, God is the judge, and the audience or Heaven is the court

32. "and not by faith only" — καὶ οὐκ ἐκ πίστεως μόνον (*kai ouk ek pisteos monon*): οὐκ (ouk) is an emphatic NO, ἐκ (*ek*) means out of, πίστεως is faith, and μόνον (*monon*) means by itself, only, or merely alone

SYNOPSIS

"Hypocrites!" That's what Jesus called the Pharisees and Sadducees who didn't practice what they preached. Where would He get such a word? It was likely from His personal experience of going to the theater in the nearby town of Sepphoris when He was growing up. Actors that performed on stage were called *hypocrites* by the Greeks. These mask-wearing performers had memorized all the lines and knew all the lingo to play their part with precision.

When Jesus called the Pharisees and Sadducees *hypocrites*, He was literally saying, "I know who you are! You've learned all the lingo of Scripture and memorized all the religious lines, and you'll say anything to get the applause of people. But you don't mean a word of it. You're just a bunch of mask-wearing pretenders. Your faith is fake, phony, and bogus!"

Well, if there's a fake faith, there has to be a *real faith*. There are numerous examples in Scripture of people with real faith. Paul said that Timothy had a real, "unfeigned faith" (*see* 2 Timothy 1:5), which means he was *without hypocrisy* just like the many Old Testament heroes of faith — including Abraham, the father of faith who we'll focus on in this lesson.

The emphasis of this lesson:

Abraham's faith was demonstrated by his actions. The fact that he obeyed God immediately and took the necessary steps to offer his son Isaac as a sacrifice was indisputable proof of his real faith. And God credited his faith — which was backed by his actions — as righteousness.

A BRIEF REVIEW OF LESSON 3

Real Faith Is Visibly Evident

If your faith is real, it will come with actions. James, the half-brother of Jesus hammered home this point in the second chapter of his letter to First-Century believers. He said, "Even so faith, if it hath not works, is dead, being alone. Yea, a man may say, Thou hast faith, and I have works: shew me thy faith without thy works, and I will shew thee my faith by my works" (James 2:17,18).

We saw that the word "shew," which appears twice in verse 18, is the Greek word *deiknumi*, and it depicts *something outwardly observable or done visibly to authenticate, prove, or guarantee something to onlookers.* This means that when real faith is operating, it is *demonstrated*, *illustrated*, and vividly *proven* by works. If you don't have any works, there is something fatally wrong with your faith.

Demons Have 'Fake Faith'

James took his example even further by saying, "Thou believest that there is one God; thou doest well: the devils also believe, and tremble" (James 2:19). In the original Greek text, this verse is very direct. For example, the words "thou believest" in Greek is *su pisteueis*, which would better be translated as a question with an element of speculation. It is the equivalent of saying, "So you say you believe there is one God, do you?"

Then he added, "…Thou doest well.…" In Greek, the word "doest" is *poieo*, which means *do*, but the tense here denotes ongoing action — *you are doing*. The word "well" is the Greek word *kalos*, and it means *good, beautiful, super*, or *superb*. Taken together, James was saying, "So you say you believe, do you? Well, you're doing pretty good. But the devils also believe and tremble."

We saw that the word "devils" is the Greek word *daimonion*, which depicts *evil spirits, demons*, or *devils*. James said that evil spirits and demons "believe," which is the Greek word *pistis*, the New Testament word for *faith*. As shocking as it may seem, this verse informs us that demon spirits have a *rock-solid belief* in God and Jesus. In fact, their faith is so strong they "tremble" at the thought of Him.

In Greek, the word "tremble" is *phrisso*, and it pictures *trembling* or *tremors*. It means *to shudder, to be struck with extreme fear, to be horrified*; or *to be panicked*. That's how the demons reacted when Jesus showed up on the scene in the gospel accounts. They were terrified in His presence and begged Him not to torment them before their appointed time of judgement.

Essentially, what James told us is that if we have faith *without* or *apart from* works, we're in the same category as demons. They also believe and even tremble at the name of Jesus and the knowledge of God. But that kind of faith is dead and doesn't change anything.

Faith Existing Apart From Works Is Unprofitable

Without hesitation, James reiterated in verse 20 what he stated in verse 17: "But wilt thou know, O vain man, that faith without works is dead?" (James 2:20) The word "vain" is the Greek word *kenos*, and it depicts *something that is empty, void*, or *wasted*. It denotes *emptiness* or *shallowness*, and in this verse it describes *an empty-headed, shallow thinker*. Thus, a literal translation of this passage would be, "Wilt thou know, O empty-headed shallow thinker, that faith without works is dead."

We learned that the word "that" is the Greek word *hoti*, which points to *an important, concrete conclusion*. The word "without" is the Greek word *choris*, which means *to be outside of something* or *apart from something*. And the Greek word for "works" is *erga*, which describes *works, deeds, activity,* or *outward accompanying actions.* Taking all these meanings into account, James was telling us that *faith existing outside of works or outward actions is dead.*

The Greek word for "dead" here is not *nekros* but *argos*, which means *unprofitable, lazy, worthless, unprovable,* or even *injurious.* This means faith apart from accompanying works is *unprofitable, lazy, worthless,* and *unprovable.* It can also be *injurious* to the health of the Church and the advancement of God's Kingdom. Think about it. When people say, "My faith is a private matter that I don't talk about or demonstrate publicly," it gives others the wrong impression of what faith is. *Silent faith that is missing in action is dead and worthless.* Real faith is never silent and always comes with outward actions.

Abraham Had Real Faith

After presenting his hypothetical situation comparing the man of real faith vs. the man of fake faith, James turns our attention to the example of Abraham when he stated:

> **Was not Abraham our father justified by works, when he had offered Isaac his son upon the altar? Seest thou how faith wrought with his works, and by works was faith made perfect? And the scripture was fulfilled which saith, Abraham believed God, and it was imputed unto him for righteousness: and he was called the Friend of God. Ye see then how that by works a man is justified, and not by faith only.**
> **— James 2:21-24**

First of all, James asked the question, "Was not Abraham our father justified by works…" (James 2:21). The word "justified" here is the Greek word *dikaioo*, from the term *dike*, referring to *a judicial verdict.* Here, it is *a verdict that declares one to be legally approved, made right, or declared to be righteous by the court.* It pictures *one who has an upright standing before a court of law.* In this case, God is the judge, and the audience or Heaven is the court.

This verse tells us that Abraham received a verdict from the courts of Heaven that declared him *legally approved* and *righteous.* And according to the original Greek text, it was *out of* or *because of his works.* They gave clear proof of his confession of faith. What outward actions verified Abraham's faith? The Bible says "…When he had offered Isaac his son upon the altar" (James 2:21).

In Greek, the word "offered" is *anaphero*, and it carries the idea of *a sacrifice that is premeditated, carefully carried out, and performed with intention*. Thus, when Abraham brought his sacrificial offering to God, it was a sacrifice following premeditated planning and determined intention to give what God asked him to surrender, which in this case was his son Isaac.

The phrase "his son" in the original Greek actually says *the son of his*, and because it includes a definite article — *the* son — it indicates *the son Abraham loved so dearly*. This word "son" is derived from the Greek word *huois*, which describes *a son, by birth or adoption; one who shares the same nature as a father, and who possesses the legal rights to his father's inheritance.*

Abraham offered his son Isaac "upon the altar." This word "upon" is the Greek word *epi*, which literally means *upon* or *on top of*. The Greek word for "altar" is *thusiasterion*, and it describes *an altar for slaying and burning of a sacrificial animal*. It can also denote *a meeting place between God and a worshiper* or *a holy point of consecration and surrender*.

The Genesis Account of Abraham Offering Isaac

When Abraham was nearly 120 years of age, God commanded him to do the hardest thing he had ever done in his life. The Bible says:

> And he [God] said, Take now thy son, thine only son Isaac, whom thou lovest, and get thee into the land of Moriah; and offer him there for a burnt offering upon one of the mountains which I will tell thee of.
>
> And Abraham rose up early in the morning, and saddled his ass, and took two of his young men with him, and Isaac his son, and clave the wood for the burnt offering, and rose up, and went unto the place of which God had told him.
>
> Then on the third day Abraham lifted up his eyes, and saw the place afar off. And Abraham said unto his young men, Abide ye here with the ass; and I and the lad will go yonder and worship, and come again to you.
> — **Genesis 22:2-5**

Notice, how Abraham didn't drag his feet but got up early and did what God asked him to do. In his words to his young servants, you can hear that his faith was engaged with his actions. He said, "...I and the lad will go yonder and worship, and come again to you" (Genesis 22:5). He believed that even if he offered up his son Isaac on the altar, God would raise him from the dead. The Bible goes on to say:

> And Abraham took the wood of the burnt offering, and laid it upon Isaac his son; and he took the fire in his hand, and a knife; and they went both of them together.
>
> And Isaac spake unto Abraham his father, and said, My father: and he said, Here am I, my son. And he said, Behold the fire and the wood: but where is the lamb for a burnt offering?
>
> And Abraham said, My son, God will provide himself a lamb for a burnt offering: so they went both of them together.
> — Genesis 22:6-8

From these verses we see that Abraham did not slow his pace or deviate from God's directive. Rather, he was actively moving in faith and declaring faith with the words of his mouth. Scripture then says:

> And they came to the place which God had told him of; and Abraham built an altar there, and laid the wood in order, and bound Isaac his son, and laid him on the altar upon the wood.
>
> And Abraham stretched forth his hand, and took the knife to slay his son. And the angel of the Lord called unto him out of heaven, and said, Abraham, Abraham: and he said, Here am I.
>
> And he said, Lay not thine hand upon the lad, neither do thou any thing unto him: for now I know that thou fearest God, seeing thou hast not withheld thy son, thine only son from me.
>
> And Abraham lifted up his eyes, and looked, and behold behind him a ram caught in a thicket by his horns: and Abraham went and took the ram, and offered him up for a burnt offering in the stead of his son.
> — Genesis 22:9-13

That day Abraham proved he was serious about his faith. Instead of just *saying* he believed God, he proved that he believed God by his actions. His faith was visible and came with accompanying actions.

Faith Works Together With Works

Returning to James' observations of Abraham's life, he wrote, "Seest thou how faith wrought with his works, and by works was faith made perfect?" (James 2:22) There are several key words in this verse, including the first word "seest." It is the Greek word *blepo*, which means *to watch, to see, to behold,* or *to be aware.* This word was often intended to jolt and jar a listener or viewer to perk up and really listen to what is being said or to what is being seen.

The word "how" is the Greek word *hoti*, and it points to *something concrete.* In this case, it points to Abraham's "faith." Again, this word "faith" is the Greek word *pistis*, the New Testament word for *faith* denoting *one who is persuaded* or *convinced to the core.* Abraham's rock-solid belief enabled him to "…wrought with his works, and by works was faith made perfect" (James 2:22).

The words "wrought with" are a translation of the Greek word *sunergeo*, which means *working with, cooperating with,* or *to work together with.* It pictures *two or more people or components working together to mutually accomplish a task.* Hence, it depicts *faith* working with and assisting *works.*

The Bible says, "…And by works was faith made perfect?" (James 2:22). In Greek, the phrase "and by works" means *and out of the midst of works* or *and in participation with works.* "Made perfect" — the Greek word *teleioo* — means *to reach its end; to reach the end-aim; to function at full strength;* or *to become full-grown.* It pictures transitioning from being youthful and immature to one who is full-grown and mature. It can also denote spiritually mature individuals who are living in accordance with the will of God.

Abraham Was Declared To Be the Righteous Friend of God

James went on to say, "And the scripture was fulfilled which saith, Abraham believed God, and it was imputed unto him for righteousness: and he was called the Friend of God" (James 2:23). When it says that Abraham *believed* God, the word "believed" is again the Greek word *pistis*, which describes *one who is persuaded* or has *a rock-solid belief*. Moreover, the term "imputed" is a form of the Greek word *logidzomai*, which means *to mathematically count, calculate, tabulate*, or *to make a conclusion*. It was used early in the bookkeeping world to portray the idea of a balance sheet or a profit-and-loss statement that a bookkeeper prepared at the end of the month or year. Thus, the word *logidzomai* — translated here as "imputed" — means *to make a calculation; to count, decide, deem, impute*, or *reckon*.

When God saw Abraham's actions cooperating with his faith, God *calculated* and *counted* them as "righteousness," which in Greek is the word *dikaiosune*, from the word *dike*, the word for *a judicial verdict*. Here, it is *a verdict that declares one to be legally approved, made right, or declared to be righteous by the court*. In this case, God is the judge, and the audience or Heaven is the court; the Great Judge and the Court of Heaven imputed to Abraham an approved status and righteousness.

Furthermore, Scripture says that Abraham was "called the Friend of God." The word "called" here is the Greek word *kaleo*, which is past tense and carries the idea of being *called* or *invited*. It can also mean to be *called by others*. The word "Friend" in Greek is *philos*, which describes *a friend* or *someone dearly loved and prized in a personal, intimate way*. That is what Abraham was to God — a trusted confidant and highly valued friend that God held dear in a close bond of personal affection.

We Are Justified by Faith and Works

James wraps up his examination of Abraham by saying, "Ye see then how that by works a man is justified, and not by faith only" (James 2:24). The word "see" is the Greek word *horao*, and it means *to see; behold; perceive; delightfully view; to look with the intent to examine;* or *to fully view*. It can also mean *to experience* or *to know from personal observation*.

James was asking his readers — which includes *us* — to *fully view, examine*, and *perceive* "...that by works a man is justified, and not by faith only" (James 2:24). The word "that" is once again the Greek word *hoti*, which *points to a conclusion*, and the conclusion it points to is *by works a man is justified*. In Greek, the phrase "by works" is *ex ergon*, which could be translated *out of works, out of the midst of works*, or *in the midst of works*.

It is out of the midst of works that we are "...justified, and not by faith only." This word "justified" is again the Greek word *dikaioo*, which is from the word *dike*, describing *a judicial verdict*. Again, it *indicates a verdict that declares one to be legally approved, made right, or declared to be righteous by the court.* In this case, God is the judge, and the audience or Heaven is the court.

This brings us to the phrase "and not by faith only," which in Greek is *kai ouk ek pisteos monon*, a compound of several words. The first is the word *ouk*, which is *an emphatic NO*; second is the word *ek*, which means *out of*; third is a form of the word *pistis*, which is the New Testament word for "faith" and describes *one who is persuaded* or *a rock-solid belief.* The fourth word is *monon*, which means *by itself, only*, or *merely alone.*

Again, when real faith is in operation, it will always be accompanied by actions. In our final lesson, we will look at what James has to say about the extraordinary faith exhibited through Rahab the harlot.

STUDY QUESTIONS

Study to shew thyself approved unto God, a workman that needeth not to be ashamed, rightly dividing the word of truth.
— 2 Timothy 2:15

1. According to Genesis 22:3, Abraham promptly obeyed God by rising early in the morning to carry out His instructions. How does the Bible say you will be blessed when you obey God? Check out these verses for some powerful insights.
   - Isaiah 1:19
   - 1 Kings 3:14
   - Deuteronomy 28:1-13
   - James 1:25
   - 1 John 3:22

2. Abraham left us a vivid example of what faith and corresponding works looks like. How does Romans 4:18-25 encourage you to keep trusting God to honor His Word even in the midst of seemingly impossible situations? What connection between Abraham and Jesus is revealed in Galatians 3:6-9,14,16,29, and how does it affect you?

PRACTICAL APPLICATION

But be ye doers of the word, and not hearers only,
deceiving your own selves.
—James 1:22

1. Of all the teachings you've heard and the studies you've done on Abraham, what is it about his life that you most appreciate? In what ways can you personally identify with his example?

2. The greatest test of Abraham's life was when God asked him to sacrifice what he loved most — his cherished son Isaac. What things has God asked *you* to surrender to Him throughout your journey of faith? What was the most difficult sacrifice He has asked of you? How has He blessed your obedience?

LESSON 5

TOPIC

The Example of Rahab's Faith

SCRIPTURES

1. **James 2:22-26** — Seest thou how faith wrought with his works, and by works was faith made perfect? And the scripture was fulfilled which saith, Abraham believed God, and it was imputed unto him for righteousness: and he was called the Friend of God. Ye see then how that by works a man is justified, and not by faith only. Likewise also was not Rahab the harlot justified by works, when she had received the messengers, and had sent them out another way? For as the body without the spirit is dead, so faith without works is dead also.

2. **Joshua 2:1-11** — And Joshua the son of Nun sent out of Shittim two men to spy secretly, saying, Go view the land, even Jericho. And they went, and came into an harlot's house, named Rahab, and lodged there. And it was told the king of Jericho, saying, Behold, there came men in hither to night of the children of Israel to search out the country. And the king of Jericho sent unto Rahab, saying, Bring forth the men that are come to thee, which are entered into thine house: for they be come to search out all the country. And the woman took the

two men, and hid them, and said thus, There came men unto me, but I wist not whence they were: and it came to pass about the time of shutting of the gate, when it was dark, that the men went out: whither the men went I wot not: pursue after them quickly; for ye shall overtake them. But she had brought them up to the roof of the house, and hid them with the stalks of flax, which she had laid in order upon the roof. And the men pursued after them the way to Jordan unto the fords: and as soon as they which pursued after them were gone out, they shut the gate. And before they were laid down, she came up unto them upon the roof; and she said unto the men, I know that the Lord hath given you the land, and that your terror is fallen upon us, and that all the inhabitants of the land faint because of you. For we have heard how the Lord dried up the water of the Red sea for you, when ye came out of Egypt; and what ye did unto the two kings of the Amorites, that were on the other side Jordan, Sihon and Og, whom ye utterly destroyed. And as soon as we had heard these things, our hearts did melt, neither did there remain any more courage in any man, because of you: for the Lord your God, he is God in heaven above, and in earth beneath.

3. **Hebrews 11:31** — By faith the harlot Rahab perished not with them that believed not, when she had received the spies with peace.

GREEK WORDS

1. "seest" — βλέπω (*blepo*): to watch, to see, to behold, to be aware; often intended to jolt and jar a listener or viewer to perk up and really listen to what is being said or to what is being seen

2. "how" — ὅτι (*hoti*): that; points to a conclusion

3. "faith" — πίστις (*pistis*): the New Testament word for faith; the root describes one who is persuaded; conveys the idea of that which is faithful, reliable, loyal, and steadfast; pictures that which is trust-worthy, dependable, dedicated, constant, reliable, unfailing, and unwavering; a rock-solid belief; convinced to the core

4. "wrought with" — συνεργέω (*sunergeo*): tense, working with; meaning to cooperate with; to work together with; to assist with; pictures two or more people or components working together to mutually accom-plish a task

5. "and by works" — καὶ ἐκ τῶν ἔργων (*kai ek ton ergon*): and out of the midst of works; and from works; and in participation with works

6. "made perfect" — τελειόω (*teleioo*): to reach its end; to reach the end-aim; to function at full strength; to become full-grown; pictures transitioning from being youthful and immature to one who is full-grown and mature; denotes spiritually mature individuals who are living in accordance with the will of God

7. "believed" — πίστις (*pistis*): the New Testament word for faith; the root describes one who is persuaded; a rock-solid belief; convinced to the core

8. "imputed" — λογίζομαι (*logidzomai*): to mathematically count, calculate, or tabulate or to make a conclusion; used early in the bookkeeping world to portray the idea of a balance sheet or a profit-and-loss statement that a bookkeeper prepared at the end of the month or year; to make a calculation; to count, decide, deem, impute, reckon

9. "righteousness" — δικαιοσύνη (*dikaiosune*): from δίκη (*dike*), a judicial verdict; here, a verdict that declares one to be legally approved, made right, or declared to be righteous by the court; to have an upright standing before a court of law; in this case, God is the judge, and the audience or Heaven is the court; the Great Judge and the Court of Heaven imputed him to a status of approval and righteousness

10. "called" — καλέω (*kaleo*): past tense; called or invited; or called by others

11. "Friend" — φίλος (*philos*): friend; someone dearly loved and prized in a personal, intimate way; a trusted confidant; one held dear in a close bond of personal affection; a highly valued friend; a close associate

12. "see" — ὁράω (*horao*): to see; to perceive; to observe

13. "that" — ὅτι (*hoti*): points to a conclusion

14. "by works" — ἐξ ἔργων (*ex ergon*): out of works; out of the midst of works; in the midst of works

15. "and not by faith only" — καὶ οὐκ ἐκ πίστεως μόνον (*kai ouk ek pisteos monon*): οὐκ (*ouk*) is an emphatic NO, ἐκ (*ek*) means out of, πίστεως is faith, and μόνον (*monon*) means by itself, only, or merely alone

16. "likewise" — ὁμοίως (*homoios*): likewise; in a similar manner; equally

17. "Rahab" — Canaanite prostitute in Jericho who worked with Hebrews spies to deliver them; an ancestor of Christ

18. "harlot" — πόρνη (*porne*): a prostitute; a woman who sells herself for sexual services

19. "justified" — δικαιόω (*dikaioo*): from δίκη (*dike*), referring to a judicial verdict; here, a verdict that declares one to be legally approved, made right, or declared to be righteous by the court; to have an upright standing before a court of law; in this case, God is the judge, and the audience or Heaven is the court

20. "by works" — ἐξ ἔργων (*ex ergon*): out of works; in the midst of her works; accompanying actions

21. "received" — ὑποδέχομαι (*hupodechomai*): to take under; to receive under; to readily and warmly receive under her roof

22. "for as" — ὥσπερ (*husper*): just as; even as

23. "body" — σῶμα (*soma*): the natural, physical body

24. "without" — χωρὶς (*choris*): to be outside of something, such as someone who lives outside the perimeters of a city; a comparison between being outside or inside something; depicts someone who is out of, not in, a specific location; primarily, to be on the outside

25. "spirit" — πνεῦμα (*pneuma*): spirit; here, human spirit and inner life force

26. "dead" — νεκρός (*nekros*): a lifeless corpse; a cadaver with no life left in it; a body disconnected to life; a corpse

27. "so" — οὕτως (*houtos*): in a similar way; in like fashion

28. "without" — χωρὶς (*choris*): to be outside of something, such as someone who lives outside the perimeters of a city; a comparison between being outside or inside something; depicts someone who is out of, not in, a specific location; primarily, to be on the outside

29. "works" — ἔργα (*erga*): works, deeds, or activity, outward accompanying actions; outward proof and evidence of faith

30. "dead" — νεκρός (*nekros*): a lifeless corpse; a cadaver with no life left in it; a body disconnected to life; a corpse

SYNOPSIS

Jesus had (and has) the amazing ability to see people as they really are. That's why when He looked at the Pharisees and Sadducees, He called them hypocrites because He knew they lacked real faith. Using their example of what *not* to be, He told His disciples, "For I tell you, unless your righteousness (your uprightness and right standing with God) is more than that of the scribes and Pharisees, you will never enter the kingdom of heaven" (Matthew 5:20 *AMPC*).

Through the apostle Paul, the Holy Spirit makes this sobering statement: "Check up on yourselves. Are you really Christians? Do you pass the test? Do you feel Christ's presence and power more and more within you? Or are you just pretending to be Christians when actually you aren't at all?" (2 Corinthians 13:5 *TLB*) Keep these thought-provoking questions in mind as you dive into this final lesson on *Real Faith vs. Fake Faith*.

The emphasis of this lesson:

Rahab was a Canaanite prostitute in Jericho who worked with Hebrew spies to protect and deliver them. The Bible says she operated in faith in the same way Abraham did, and as a result, she was justified and declared righteous in God's eyes.

A BRIEF REVIEW OF LESSON 4

Faith and Works Are Partners

In our last lesson, we saw how faith was visibly at work in the life of Abraham. James calls our attention to his example saying, "Was not Abraham our father justified by works, when he had offered Isaac his son upon the altar? Seest thou how faith wrought with his works, and by works was faith made perfect?" (James 2:21,22)

The word "seest" is the Greek word *blepo*, which means *to watch, to see, to behold*, or *to be aware*. It was often used in the Greek language to jolt and jar a listener to perk up his ears and really hear what is about to be said because it is so important. James' use of this word is the equivalent of him saying, "Are you really listening? Do you understand? Do you see how faith is wrought with works?"

In Greek, the phrase "wrought with" is *sunergeo*, which means *working with, cooperating with*, or *to work together with*. It pictures *two or more people or components working together to mutually accomplish a task*. This lets us know that faith alone doesn't work; it has to have a partner. And the partner of faith is actions or accompanying works.

Faith-Filled Actions Produce Spiritual Maturity

Abraham had faith and he had works, and the Bible says, "…And by works was faith made perfect" (James 2:22). In Greek, the phrase "and by works" is *kai ek ton ergon*, which literally means *and out of the midst of works* or *and in participation with works*. In other words, his faith was not alone. It was out of the cooperation of his works that his faith was *made perfect*.

"Made perfect" is a translation of the Greek word *teleioo*, and it means *to reach its end, to reach the end-aim*, or *to function at full strength*. It pictures transitioning from being youthful and immature to *one who is full-grown and mature*. It can also denote spiritually mature individuals who are living in accordance with the will of God.

Abraham had faith in God, but when he put actions to his faith, it developed him into spiritual manhood. That is why James went on to tell us, "And the scripture was fulfilled which saith, Abraham believed God, and it was imputed unto him for righteousness: and he was called the Friend of God" (James 2:23).

God Reckoned Abraham To Be Righteous

The word "believed" is derived from the Greek word *pistis*, which is the New Testament word for *faith*. It describes *one who is totally persuaded* and has *a rock-solid belief*. That is who Abraham was. He had become convinced to the core of God's faithfulness, and because of his faith, God imputed to him righteousness.

The term "imputed" is a form of the Greek word *logidzomai*, which means *to mathematically count, calculate, tabulate*, or *to make a conclusion*. This word was used early in the bookkeeping world to portray the idea of a balance sheet or a profit-and-loss statement that a bookkeeper prepared at the end of the month or year. Thus, the word *logidzomai* — translated here as "imputed" — means *to make a calculation; to count, decide, deem, impute*, or *reckon*.

When God saw Abraham's actions that accompanied his faith, He calculated and counted them as "righteousness." This is the Greek word *dikaiosune*, from the word *dike*, which describes *a judicial verdict*. Here, it is *a verdict that declares one to be legally approved, made right, or declared to be righteous by the court*. In this case, God is the judge, and the audience or Heaven is the court; the Great Judge and the Court of Heaven imputed to him an approved status of righteousness.

Abraham Was Called God's Friend

Furthermore, Scripture says that Abraham was "…called the Friend of God" (James 2:23). The word "called" here is the Greek word *kaleo*, which is past tense and carries the idea of being *called* or *invited*. It can also mean to be *called by others*. In this verse, *kaleo* could mean Abraham was called to be a friend of God, or he was called a friend of God by others. Indeed, when you walk in faith, your accompanying actions qualify you to be God's friend and to be called His friend by others.

The word "Friend" is the Greek word *philos*, and it describes *a friend*, or *someone dearly loved and prized in a personal, intimate way*. It could also be translated *a close associate*. That's what Abraham was to God — a trusted confidant, a close associate, and highly valued friend that God held dear in a close bond of personal affection.

'By Works, Not By Faith Only'

James went on to say, "Ye see then how that by works a man is justified, and not by faith only" (James 2:24). Interestingly, the word "how" doesn't appear in the original Greek text. Instead, it merely reads, "Ye see then that…." The word "that" is the Greek word *hoti*, which *points to a specific conclusion*. The word "see" is the Greek word *horao*, and it means *to see; behold; perceive;* or *delightfully view*. The use of these words tells us that we can make a personal observation of Abraham's actions in the Scriptures and come to a conclusion "…*that* by works a man is justified, and not by faith only."

In Greek, the phrase "by works" is *ex ergon*, which could be translated *out of works, out of the midst of works*, or *in the midst of works*. It is out of the midst of works that Abraham and all of us are justified "…and not by faith only."

This phrase "and not by faith only" is a compound of four Greek words: the word *ouk*, which is *an emphatic NO*; the word *ek*, which means *out of*; and a form of the word *pistis*, which is the New Testament word for "faith," describing *one who is persuaded* or *a rock-solid belief*. The fourth word is *monon*, which means *by itself, only*, or *merely alone*. When all these words are joined together, it means *absolutely and emphatically not by faith alone; not by faith by itself*. In other words, when real faith is operating, it will have accompanying actions.

Rahab Operated in Faith
Just As Abraham Did and Was 'Justified'

Now, you may be thinking, *Well, I'm just not as spiritual as Abraham, and I just don't know if I can operate in that kind of faith.* If that thought has crossed your mind, James offers this additional example of faith: "Likewise also was not Rahab the harlot justified by works, when she had received the messengers, and had sent them out another way?" (James 2:25)

The word "likewise" here is the Greek word *homoios*, which means *likewise, in a similar manner*, or *equally*. This word connects the example of Rahab with the previous example of Abraham and tells us that she operated in faith *equally* as he did. Please realize that Rahab was a Canaanite prostitute in Jericho who worked with Hebrew spies to protect and deliver them.

The word "harlot" in verse 25 is the Greek word *porne*, and it describes *a prostitute; a woman who sells herself for sexual services*. Yet despite her sinful past, because she operated in faith and protected the two Israelite spies, the Bible says she was "justified." Again, "justified" is the Greek word *dikaioo*, from the word *dike*, referring to *a judicial verdict*. Here, *it is a verdict that declares one to be legally approved, made right, or declared to be righteous by the court.* Furthermore, it means *to have an upright standing before a court of law*, and in this case, God is the judge, and the audience or Heaven is the court.

Therefore, in the eyes of God and the court of Heaven, Rahab was legally approved and declared righteous. How? "By works" — which is the Greek word *ex ergon*, meaning *out of works* or *in the midst of her works*. This is a description of accompanying actions. Rahab didn't just say she believed in God; she backed up her words with works. She "…received the messengers, and had sent them out another way" (James 2:25).

The word "received" is a translation of the Greek word *hupodechomai*, which means *to take under, to receive under,* or *to readily and warmly receive under her roof*. Rahab risked her life and the lives of her family by hiding and protecting the two Israelite men. Her actions proved the quality of her faith in the God of Israel.

Rahab's Story As Recorded in the Book of Joshua

The city of Jericho was Rahab's hometown. It was also the first city west of the Jordan River that Joshua and the nation of Israel went to war against in their conquest of the Promise Land. The Bible says:

> **And Joshua the son of Nun sent out of Shittim two men to spy secretly, saying, Go view the land, even Jericho. And they went, and came into an harlot's house, named Rahab, and lodged there.**
>
> **And it was told the king of Jericho, saying, Behold, there came men in hither to night of the children of Israel to search out the country.**
>
> **And the king of Jericho sent unto Rahab, saying, Bring forth the men that are come to thee, which are entered into thine house: for they be come to search out all the country.**
>
> **And the woman took the two men, and hid them....**
> — Joshua 2:1-4

Rahab's actions in verse 4 are the first visible sign of her faith. Scripture says she hid the Israelite spies and in so doing protected them from being caught by the king. Her faith in God's power and might working through the people of Israel was demonstrated by her deeds. When the king's entourage arrived with their interrogation, Rahab turned to them and said:

> **...There came men unto me, but I wist not whence they were: And it came to pass about the time of shutting of the gate, when it was dark, that the men went out: whither the men went I wot not: pursue after them quickly; for ye shall overtake them.**
>
> **But she had brought them up to the roof of the house, and hid them with the stalks of flax, which she had laid in order upon the roof.**
>
> **And the men pursued after them the way to Jordan unto the fords: and as soon as they which pursued after them were gone out, they shut the gate.**
> — Joshua 2:4-7

By hiding the spies and fabricating a story of their whereabouts, Rahab diverted the king and his henchmen on a wild goose chase. This gave the Israelites the time they would need to eventually slip away unnoticed and make it back to their camp. The Bible goes on to say:

> **And before they were laid down, she came up unto them upon the roof;**
>
> **And she said unto the men, I know that the Lord hath given you the land, and that your terror is fallen upon us, and that all the inhabitants of the land faint because of you.**
>
> **For we have heard how the Lord dried up the water of the Red sea for you, when ye came out of Egypt; and what ye did unto the two kings of the Amorites, that were on the other side Jordan, Sihon and Og, whom ye utterly destroyed.**
>
> **And as soon as we had heard these things, our hearts did melt, neither did there remain any more courage in any man, because of you: for the Lord your God, he is God in heaven above, and in earth beneath.**
>
> **— Joshua 2:8-11**

Wow! What a declaration of faith! Rahab — the Canaanite prostitute — said, "…The Lord your God, he is God in heaven above, and in earth beneath" (Joshua 2:11). She had real faith in the One True God, and that faith was demonstrated by her courageous actions to hide and protect the two Israelite spies. And it was her demonstrated faith that saved her life. The writer of Hebrews said, "By faith the harlot Rahab perished not with them that believed not, when she had received the spies with peace" (Hebrews 11:31). Friend, if Rahab the harlot can act in faith, so can you!

Actions Prove Faith

James concludes the second chapter of his book by saying, "For as the body without the spirit is dead, so faith without works is dead also" (James 2:26). In this passage, the words "for as" is the Greek word *husper*, which means *just as* or *even as*. And the word "body" in Greek is *soma*, and refers to *the natural, physical body*.

James said, "*Just as the physical body* without the spirit is dead, so faith without works is dead also" (James 2:26). The word "without" is the

Greek word *choris*, which means *to be outside of something*. In this case, it is describing the physical body being *outside of* or *apart from* the spirit.

The Greek word for "spirit" here is *pneuma*, and it describes *a person's spirit*. Here, it signifies *the human spirit* and *inner life force*. When the physical body is apart from or outside of a person's human spirit, he or she is dead. The word "dead" in James 2:26 is the Greek word *nekros*, which we saw earlier. It describes *a lifeless corpse* or *a cadaver with no life left in it*. It is *a body disconnected to life*. There is no breath in the lungs, no heartbeat in the chest, and no pulse in the wrist.

James declared that just as the physical body apart from the human spirit is a lifeless corpse, "...So faith without works is dead also" (James 2:26). The word "so" here is the Greek word *houtos*, which means *in a similar way* or *in like fashion*. The word "without" is again the Greek word *choris*, meaning *to be outside of something*. Moreover, the word "works" in Greek is *erga*, which describes *works, deeds, activity*, or *outward accompanying actions* that are proof and evidence of faith. And the word "dead" is the Greek word *nekros*, the term for *a lifeless corpse*.

Putting all these meanings together, we see that James is restating for a third time the truth he's been pounding home all through his second chapter: "Faith that is apart from or outside of works (accompanying actions) is like a cadaver with no life left in it." If you see someone who claims to have faith but they have no actions to prove it, it is the equivalent of looking at a corpse in a casket.

Clearly, these are powerful, sobering words to chew on. Nevertheless, it is imperative that we not deceive ourselves regarding the kind of faith we have. As we close this study, consider once more these instructions from Paul to the Corinthian church and all believers in every generation: "Test yourselves to make sure you are solid in the faith. Don't drift along taking everything for granted. Give yourselves regular checkups. You need firsthand evidence, not mere hearsay, that Jesus Christ is in you. Test it out. If you fail the test, do something about it" (2 Corinthians 13:5 *MSG*).

STUDY QUESTIONS

Study to shew thyself approved unto God, a workman that
needeth not to be ashamed, rightly dividing the word of truth.
— 2 Timothy 2:15

1. What new insights did you learn from this lesson about Rahab and the strong faith she demonstrated? What do her words in Joshua 2:9-11 say to you about her view of God?

2. What did Rahab ask the Israelite spies to give her in return for helping them (*see* Joshua 2:12,13)? What did the two men say in response to her request, and what did she need to do in order to receive what she asked for (*see* Joshua 2:14-21)?

3. What happened to Rahab and her family when the Israelites conquered Jericho (*see* Joshua 6:22,23,25)? What ultimate blessing did God give Rahab for actively aligning herself with Him? (*See* Matthew 1:1-16, especially verse 5.) What does her example speak to you personally about actively doing God's will?

PRACTICAL APPLICATION

> But be ye doers of the word, and not hearers only,
> deceiving your own selves.
> —James 1:22

1. As we wrap up this series, take time to evaluate your own faith. Be honest: Is your faith like that of the Sadducees and Pharisees? Do you know and speak all the right "spiritual lines" but your heart is not in it? Are you merely speaking words of faith but lacking the authenticating actions to back it up?

2. Consider praying David's prayer found in Psalm 139:23,24 in *The Passion Translation*:

God, I invite your searching gaze into my heart. Examine me through and through; find out everything that may be hidden within me. Put me to the test and sift through all my anxious cares. See if there is any path of pain I'm walking on, and lead me back to your glorious, everlasting way — the path that brings me back to you.

Be still and listen. What is the Holy Spirit speaking to you? What needs to change in your life? And what practical steps do you have to take to see change take place?

Notes

Notes

_____

_____

_____

_____

_____

_____

_____

_____

_____

_____

_____

_____

_____

_____

_____

_____

_____

_____

_____

_____

_____

_____

_____

_____

_____

_____

Notes